JOHN CLIFFORD

John Clifford was born in North Staffordshire in 1950 but has lived in Scotland since 1968. He began his playwriting career by translating two plays by Calderón, *The House with Two Doors* and *The Doctor of Honour*. His first original plays were written for radio: *Desert Places* (BBC Radio Scotland, 1983) and *Ending Time* (BBC Radio 3, 1984). Between 1985 and 1987 he wrote three plays for Jenny Killick at the Traverse Theatre, Edinburgh: *Losing Venice* (also staged at the Almeida Theatre, London, at the Perth Festival, Australia, at the Hong Kong Arts Festival, on tour in Sweden, and in Los Angeles), *Lucy's Play* (also seen in Aspen, Colorado and in Los Angeles) and *Playing with Fire*. *Inés de Castro* (1989) was Clifford's most recent work for the Traverse, and the production was subsequently seen at the Riverside Studios, London, and on BBC2. For TAG Theatre Company, Glasgow, he adapted *Romeo and Juliet* in 1984 and *Great Expectations* in 1988 (revived in 1989 to tour Iraq, Egypt, India, Sri Lanka and Bangladesh). He has also recently completed a schools adaptation of *Macbeth*.

Clifford has translated Lorca's *The House of Bernarda Alba* (Royal Lyceum Theatre, Edinburgh 1989), and Calderón's *Schism in England* (National Theatre and Edinburgh Festival 1989). He has also both adapted and translated Tirso de Molina's *Heaven Bent, Hell Bound* (Actors' Touring Company 1987) and *Celestina* by Fernando de Rojas for a forthcoming National Theatre production.

Most recently Clifford has completed *Santiago*, a documentary drama for Channel 4, *Quevedo*, a play for the BBC due to be screened in Autumn 1991, and the libretto for a new opera, *Anna*, with the composer Craig Armstrong. He is about to adapt *Anna Karenina* for the Sheffield Crucible.

by the same author

Inés de Castro
(in *First Run 2* edited by Kate Harwood)

Losing Venice
(in *Scot-Free* edited by Alasdair Cameron)

JOHN CLIFFORD

LIGHT IN
THE VILLAGE

NICK HERN BOOKS
London

A Nick Hern Book

Light in the Village first published in 1991 as an original paperback by Nick Hern Books, a Random Century Company, 20 Vauxhall Bridge Road, London SW1V 2SA

Front cover illustration from a photograph of a Bangladeshi woman cutting fruit, by Sean Hudson.

Set in Baskerville by 🅐 Tek Art Ltd, Addiscombe, Croydon, Surrey
Printed in Great Britain by
T.J. Press (Padstow) Ltd, Padstow, Cornwall.

British Library Cataloguing in Publication Data
Clifford, John
   Light in the village.
   I. Title
   822.914

   ISBN: 1854591258

The author gratefully acknowledges the Scottish Arts Council for contributing financially towards his research in India, and the British Council in Calcutta for their invaluable help.

Thanks also to Boro Baski, Zarin Chaudhri, Russell Colombo, Jack Craig, Nadine Harrison, Katie, Rebecca and Susie Innes, Aleema Khatoon, Shyamali Khastgir, Dr Manjumohan Mukherjee, Barry Underwood and the Nandikar Theatre Festival.

The play can be performed by 5 actors: 3 male and 2 female.

Distribution of characters:

ONE	MUKHERJEE (a landlord) A LAWYER
TWO	SITA
THREE	MUNTU (Sita's husband)
FOUR	MEENA (an old woman) KALI
FIVE	RHODES (the landlord's younger brother)

The actors are storytellers; and as such are not always confined to the single role. They will sometimes have to switch rapidly from one to the other, as the story demands. Rapidly and yet simply and naturally: as one does, telling stories.

It won't be possible to do this with changes of costume or of mask: they will have to change the language of their bodies.

And so in part the performance will be a celebration of their skills.

The space they perform in will not necessarily represent the village in which the story takes place: it is simply a place where people tell stories.

It could even be a railway station or a transit camp: and they will tell the story with whatever comes to hand.

The first performance of *Light in the Village* was given at the
Traverse Theatre, Edinburgh, on 3 August 1991.

The cast was as follows:

ONE	Benny Young
TWO	Sharon Maharaj
THREE	Okon Jones
FOUR	Sandy McDade
FIVE	Trevor Butler

Directed by Ian Brown
Designed by Tim Hatley
Lighting by Jeanine Davies
Stage management by John Davidson
Choreography by Wendy Houston
Music by Craig Armstrong
Assistant Director Andy Williams

This text went to press before the opening night and may
therefore differ slightly from the text as performed.

ACT ONE

There is a square. Inside the square there will be a circle.
This is the place to tell stories in.
The square will be oriented: to the north, the west, the east and the south.
There is a shrine, with an image of the Mother. Battered, maybe, and
blackened with smoke. There may be barbed wire.
There is earth, preferably on the floor. There is water. There is air and
there is fire.
Nothing is new. Everything is worn: battered by hard use. But not drab:
the colours on the costumes, say, may be faded, but they are still beautiful.
As the audience enter, the musicians tune up and the actors prepare.
Someone sweeps the floor. Someone prepares the costumes and the props.
Someone lights the incense. Someone draws the circle.
The actors greet the Mother. They greet each other. They greet the
audience. Music. The play begins.

ONE. The story begins.

TWO. The story begins at the beginning.

THREE. And in the beginning there was nothing at all.

FOUR. It was dead boring!

FIVE. No shops. No banks. Nothing!

ONE. It was all empty and grey.

TWO. And it all went on for ever and ever.

THREE. Mother Kali opened up her eyes.

   FOUR *becomes* MOTHER KALI.

ONE. Mother Kali opened her enormous eyes.

FIVE. And looked. And saw. And said:

KALI. This won't do.
  This won't do at all.

THREE. And she was right.

FIVE. There was no money. It was hopeless!

KALI. So this is what I did:

I created soap and I blew a bubble.
A big one. A great big one.
And it hung in the air.
It spun and it spun.
I love bubbles. So I blew another.
And another. And another.

And I said to one of them
– before it burst –
You'll do. You'll do for a world.

And it did. It was big and round and beautiful.
So I shrunk myself down
I shrunk myself down to the size of a flea
And there I was, the size of a tiny flea
Walking on the surface of the world.

It was all smooth and round.
It was all flat and vacant. Empty and grey.
Very boring.

So I stamped a little here
And I shook a little there
– like you'd shake a carpet,
Or maybe shake a rug.
So it was all ridges and furrows.
And there was your mountains
And there was your plains
And your wee hills and your valleys too
And it wasni bad, considering.

And then I felt hungry.

So I looked about, and saw this thingmi.
It was floating in the sky
Floating right beside me on beautiful white wings
So I ate it. God knows what it was.
I tore its head off
And I drank the blood.

It was delicious.
Tasted like chocolate.

And then I burped. That's your wind.
And then I had a pee and a little spit
And there's your oceans and your rivers and your lakes.

And I thought: I like this. This is good.
This is very good.

And then I squatted down had the most enormous shit.
Well, I thought, that's that. I'm off.
But it just so happened I looked down
And saw all these little creatures crawling out the dirt.
And that was you. And you. And you.
How I laughed. I'd given birth!
Look at them! I said, just look at them!
And some were hairy and some were smooth
And some had six legs. Some had four.
Some of them just had two.
Poor wee creatures.
And some of them had no legs at all.
They swam!
They were beautiful.
And I looked at you. I looked at all of you.
I looked at the grass and the trees and the deep blue sky
And it was good. It was very very good.
And then I said:
Go fuck yourselves.
And you did! You all did!
And you multiplied
And then I said
To all of you
To the birds and the fishes and the insects and the whales
The apes and the caterpillars
Marsupials and pigs
Ants and antelopes
Spiders humans striped and spotted snakes
I said
This is the earth.
This is the whole earth.
Take care of it
And remember. Remember who you are,
Where you came from. Where you're going.
Don't you forget. Remember. Remember me!

KALI *goes. A silence.* ONE *picks up the story.*

ONE. There was a village that she left behind

THREE. Somewhere in the east

TWO. An ordinary kind of place.

THREE. People grew up there, squabbled, grew old and died.

FIVE. Just like anywhere else

ONE. And in the village lived a rich man, Mukherjee

ONE *becomes* MUKHERJEE.

THREE. And a poor man, Muntu

THREE *becomes* MUNTU.

TWO. A woman called Sita

TWO *becomes* SITA.

FIVE. The rich man's brother, Rhodes

FIVE *becomes* RHODES.

FOUR. An old woman

FOUR *becomes* MEENA.

THREE. And many more besides.

FIVE. And they all lived together

MUKHERJEE. In peace and harmony,

SITA. In deep injustice,

MEENA. The way they always had,

TWO. Until one day –

MUKHERJEE. Muntu! Muntu!

MUNTU. Yes master.

MUKHERJEE. My clothes are dirty!

MUNTU. Yes master.

MUKHERJEE. Then don't just stand there.

MUNTU. No master.

MUKHERJEE. Wash them!

MUNTU. At once master.

MUKHERJEE. Tomorrow, Muntu, is the festival.
  The new year festival, Muntu.
  When we celebrate a new beginning.
  A new beginning to the world.
  Let us at least have clean clothes.

MUNTU. Yes master.

MUKHERJEE. Muntu, the world decays.

MUNTU. Yes master.

MUKHERJEE. The village empties and nothing is as it was.

MUNTU. No master.

MUKHERJEE. Wives do not obey their husbands.

MUNTU. Yes master.

MUKHERJEE. The servant no longer obeys his master.

MUNTU. No master.

MUKHERJEE. The bonds that held us all together are all being torn to shreds.

MUNTU. Yes master.

MUKHERJEE. We cannot control this, Muntu.
We cannot prevent or interrupt it.
It is all outside our power.
But we can at least have clean clothes.

MUNTU. No master.

MUKHERJEE. No Muntu?

MUNTU. I mean yes master. May I clean the clothes?

MUKHERJEE. Yes Muntu. We must have them clean. Spotlessly clean. White as snow.

MUNTU. Master I have never seen snow.

MUKHERJEE. Neither have I. We must imagine. Now go!

FOUR. And so the man began to wash the clothes.

MUNTU. Sita!
Wash the clothes!

SITA. No.

MUNTU. No?

SITA. I'm busy.

MUNTU. Then who will?

SITA. You will.

MUNTU. As always.

SITA. As always.

MUNTU *sighs and begins to wash the clothes.* SITA *works the pump.*

MUNTU. What are you doing?

SITA. Getting water.

MUNTU. The pump is broken.
Sita! It's been broken for months.

SITA. We need water!

MUNTU. But it won't give you any!

SITA. It might.
You never know.

MUNTU. But we do know Sita. We do know.

SITA *works the pump. This is an effort. Nothing happens.*

MUNTU. Other wives obey their husbands.
Other wives listen to their husband's advice.

SITA. Other wives are stupid.

MUNTU. Not stupid enough to use a broken pump.

SITA. All I want is clean water!

MEENA. If you want to get water then get it from the pond.

MUNTU. What I tell her.

SITA. It's dirty.

MEENA. It's all there is.

SITA. It makes us ill.

MEENA. Then boil it.

SITA. We haven't any fuel.

MEENA. Then make some.

SITA. I'm tired.

MEENA. Too bad.

Then SITA *wearily fetches a bucket of cow dung which she moulds into little cakes and slaps viciously onto the wall to dry.*

MEENA. It's life.

MUNTU. Exactly.

MEENA. Life is work.

MUNTU. Precisely.

And MUNTU *begins to wash the clothes. He slaps them against the stones.*

SITA. But the landlord has water!

MEENA. He is the landlord.

ONE. And the woman had no reply.
And so they worked.
The landlord also worked.

ONE becomes the landlord. He snores on a bed.

FIVE. One thing you must know

THREE. About Muntu,

TWO. About Sita,

TWO & THREE. They wanted a child.

FIVE. But Muntu was a feeble man.

FOUR. He couldni get it up.

FIVE. And when it did come up

FOUR. It never stayed up for long.

FIVE. It came

FOUR. And it went

THREE. And this was no laughing matter!

TWO. It hurt them. It hurt them both.

THREE. For in their way
They loved each other.

TWO. They never spoke about it.

THREE. They never could.

TWO. Life went by

THREE. And they tried to forget.

SITA. But I can't! I can't forget!

FOUR. And so the women worked,

ONE. And the landlord slept.

SITA. I want the land!

FOUR. Another thing. Another thing she wanted.

FOUR *becomes* MEENA.

MEENA. It doesn't do to want.

MUNTU. What I tell her.

SITA. I want the land. Our land.

MUNTU. We have no land.

SITA. The land the old man gave you,
  The land he left you in his will!

MUNTU. His sons took it back.

ONE. The landlord,

FIVE. And his brother.

ONE & FIVE. We did it together.

TWO. He came one evening with his suitcase full of tricks.

THREE. And I, poor Muntu, had just come home from the
  fields.

FIVE *becomes the brother*, RHODES.

RHODES. I have jewels! The finest pearls. Cultured pearls! From
  Glasgow! Hooped earrings! The finest quality! Jewels from
  Ratners! Cheap crap! The highest quality! And scarves! Feel
  this madam. Synthetic one hundred per cent! For gentlemen I
  have Marks and Spencer ties! A bottle of Coca Cola! A real
  bottle! Empty! The original design! 1954! A rarity! For you sir!
  Muntu! Something extra special! Whisky!

ONE *becomes* MUKHERJEE.

RHODES. Muntu. Real Scotch. Made in Japan. Have some.

MUKHERJEE. You are tired, Muntu.

RHODES. Drink.

MUKHERJEE. Have a small one.

RHODES. You don't have to pay. Not yet.

MUKHERJEE. And a man must relax.

RHODES. A man has a right to relax.

MUKHERJEE. Is it good?

RHODES. Have another. No harm in another.

MUKHERJEE. Or another after that.

RHODES. And now we can talk.

MUKHERJEE. Man to man. As friends of the family.

RHODES. About the land.

MUKHERJEE. The land my father gave you when he died.

RHODES. The land he gave you, the baby boy he rescued from the gutter.

MUKHERJEE. The land he gave you as a sign of love.
He was a sick man, Muntu. He was not himself.

RHODES. Why else would he give you anything?

MUKHERJEE. And would you take advantage of his sickness? Is that how you'd repay his kindness?

RHODES. Besides, Muntu, the land now burdens you. It fills you with care.

MUKHERJEE. For land is a source of care and worry to those who are not fit to own it.

RHODES. Give us the cares of the land. Let us take the troubles from your shoulders.

MUKHERJEE. And we will use it for the benefit of all.

RHODES. That's what you want Muntu.

MUKHERJEE. That's what's in your heart.

RHODES. You're in debt Muntu.

MUKHERJEE. In debt to us. Remember that.

RHODES. Sign the paper.

MUNTU. I cannot write.

MUKHERJEE. You do not need to.

RHODES. We will even save you that trouble.

FOUR. And the poor man was too drunk to resist.
He signed the paper.

RHODES *pockets the paper and pushes* MUNTU *over. He falls to the ground in a stupor.*

FOUR. And when he woke up he had a headache
And the rich man had the land.

SITA. And why should he want it?

MUKHERJEE. Never give anything away.
Never. Hold on. Hold on to what's your own.

MUNTU *stares ruefully at the land.*

SITA. And they've done nothing with it.

MUNTU. No.

SITA. They tricked you!

MUNTU. How could I resist?

SITA. You could say no.

MUNTU. It's not always so easy to say no.
Not when you're in debt.

SITA. How much is the debt?

MUNTU. A little. Not much. I don't know!

MEENA. A little is enough.

MUNTU. Besides, it's such a tiny patch of land.

MEENA. The most worthless land in the village.
That's why the old man gave it you.

MUNTU. Exactly. Waste ground. Full of stones. A tiny patch.
And it doesn't matter! It doesn't matter!

SITA. But it does Muntu. It does.

MUNTU. Yes.

SITA. We could have made it something.

MUNTU. Yes!

SITA. And they've done nothing with it. It's just full of weeds!

MUNTU. But it's their land. They can do what they like with it.

SITA. We should take it back.

MUNTU. We can't. I told you. I signed a paper. It is legal.

SITA. Then see a lawyer.

MUNTU. The lawyer is in town.

SITA. Then go to the town.

MUNTU. But how can I pay a lawyer?

SITA. Perhaps you won't have to.

MEENA. Lawyers charge you for breathing!

SITA. But he comes from the village. You told me. You were children together.

MUNTU. He'll have forgotten me.

SITA. You did him a favour.

MUNTU. It was nothing.
  He won't remember.

SITA. He might.

MUNTU. Besides how am I to go to the town?

SITA. You walk.

MUNTU. And how am I to walk?

SITA. On your legs!

MUNTU. The landlord never gives me a moment.

SITA. Go anyway.

MUNTU. I can't.

SITA. Just go!

MUNTU. Sita it is no use.
  You want me to be a hero. But I am not a hero!
  They have ordered me about from the minute I was born!
  Muntu do this. Muntu do that. That's been my life! It's not so easy to change a life!

SITA. I wish at least you would not crawl to them.

MUNTU. Sita when I am with them I obey them.
  I say yes master as you wish master.
  That is how it has always been.
  It's easier that way.
  I can speak one thing with my mouth
  And another with my heart.
  They cannot see my heart.
  They do not wish to see it.

And so they leave me in peace.
Do you understand? It is easier.
It makes life easier.
But you are right about the land.
They tricked me. I admit that.
If I get the chance I will see the lawyer.
I promise.
But don't expect anything to change.

MEENA. Forget the lawyer. The lawyer's a tired man in a dark
dusty room. Staring at bits of paper. There's nothing he can
do.

SITA. We should try.

MEENA. There's no sense trying.

SITA. We should protest.

MEENA. I once made a protest. Long ago. I lived in the city.
They wanted to clear us from our land. We didn't have much:
shacks we'd built from corrugated iron and biscuit boxes and
old bits of sacking. Some families still lived in pipes! But it was
something. It was all we had. And so we tried to keep it. We
thought we had nothing to lose. We came together and we
made a stand. We made ourselves banners and we sat in the
street. "Land for the landless! Homes for the homeless!" All
day long sitting and shouting in the street. And they did not
touch us. They did not dare touch us! We felt so proud. That
night we lit fires and we sang. "We shall overcome". A new
song. From America. So proud we felt. So happy and strong.
And the next day they came with whips and bulldozers and just
brushed us away. As if we were flies. They knocked down our
houses and took what little we possessed.
And then we discovered we did have something to lose.
Too late. We had lost it.

SITA. And that's the story of our towns. The story of our villages
and towns.

MEENA. The true story.

SITA. And that's why I hate this village. With its frightened faces
and its closed off minds. Where everyone is frightened because
of what they have to lose.

MUNTU. Sometimes it makes sense to be frightened.

SITA. With my first husband I was frightened all the time. I
crept around the house like a timid little mouse. I didn't want

to lose my position or my fine new clothes.
It made no difference. I lost them anyway.
And it's not the losing that's so terrible. It's not.
The fear is worse.
You think I'm mad. You both think I'm mad. Mad for wishing.
And you so sensible and sane.
But look at you! Look at the pair of you!
Muntu up to his knees in mud trying to clean his master's
clothes!

MUNTU. There's nowhere else.

SITA. That's what you always say!
And you're no better!
Spinning thread for cloth no one wants and no one will ever
buy!

MEENA. I have to work. Or my hands itch.
And besides, you never know. Someone may buy it.

SITA. Water may come out of the pump!

MEENA. This village

SITA. This village!
This village where nothing ever changes
Where everything always stays the same.

FIVE. But that day the brother came a second time

THREE. With his suitcase full of tricks.

ONE. The landlord was walking.

FOUR. A rare event.

   ONE *becomes* MUKHERJEE.

MUKHERJEE. Muntu!

   THREE *becomes* MUNTU.

MUNTU. Yes master.

MUKHERJEE. My umbrella! I will walk.

FOUR. The brothers met in the village street.

ONE. The elder one was fat.

FIVE. The younger one was thin.

ONE. The elder one puffed.

FIVE. And the younger one swaggered.

FIVE *becomes* RHODES.

RHODES. Brother! Are you well?

MUKHERJEE. No I am not!
The sun is hot!
Muntu can you not provide a better shade?

MUNTU. The umbrella is broken.

MUKHERJEE. Everything is broken!

RHODES. You can buy umbrellas in America that open by
themselves. You press a button and whish! You are sheltered
under stars and stripes! 200 dollars. 200 dollars!

MUKHERJEE. Think of that, Muntu. Think of that.

MUNTU. I cannot.

MUKHERJEE. The poor have no imagination.

RHODES. Two hundred dollars, Muntu, is more than you will
ever earn. More than you could earn in your whole life!

MUNTU. Am I worth less than an umbrella?

RHODES. In America, Muntu, they understand the proper price
of things.

MUNTU. But this is not America.

RHODES. More's the pity, Muntu. More's the pity.

MUKHERJEE. And we have not the umbrella!

RHODES. We must be patient, brother, and work towards better
things.

MUKHERJEE. In the meantime the sun remains hot.

RHODES. In America you can buy a fan. You press a button,
and whirr! You are in a refrigerator. Battery operated.

MUKHERJEE. But this is all beyond our means.

RHODES. So we extend our means. With this!

He produces a light bulb.

MUKHERJEE. What is it?

RHODES. Light!

MUKHERJEE. That is not light brother. That is a bulb.
A coloured glass bulb.

RHODES. But inside the bulb, brother, is a steel coil. Electricity
will pass through the coil and it will glow. And as it glows,
brother, it gives us light.

MUKHERJEE. Brother you are dreaming.

RHODES. Brother I am a practical man.
I do not dream.

MUKHERJEE. We have no electricity.

RHODES. We have the wires.

MUKHERJEE. We have the wires, but they are not for us.
They bring light to the town.
They pass us by. Life passes us by.
The village remains sunk in darkness and ignorance.
Wires pass over its people's heads, but they do not understand
the wires. They understand nothing but a full belly and the
cheap liquor which you so thoughtfully provide.
They heat themselves with sticks and dung.
They worship stones and the bark of certain trees.
In this village.
This dark village where no one comes.
Where no one reads.
Where there are no books, no newspapers, not even magazines!
I am the only person in this village who owns a book!
I am dying in this ignorance. This dark ignorance!
The village is dark and we need light.
Light in the village.
But the light is nowhere to be found.

RHODES. I have it in my case.

MUKHERJEE. You have a mess of wires.
That is not the light I mean.

RHODES. With this mess of wires, brother, I can connect us to
the power lines! Such a mess of wires is worth more than gold!
I will transform this village.

MUKHERJEE. Impossible.

RHODES. Brother! Have faith in me!

MUKHERJEE. Why should I have faith in you?

RHODES. I have been to America.

MUKHERJEE. I do not believe in America.

RHODES. I have seen it. I have stood on a tower and I have seen
it. A tower in Chicago!
I saw a city of light.
Light spreading in every direction.
Rivers of light. Towers of light.
Pictures of light.
Flashing pictures made of light!
Light. A city of light.

MUKHERJEE. That is not the light I mean.
And I do not think I want it.

RHODES. You would if you had seen it.
It is electricity.
A child can do the work of ten men simply by flicking a switch.
And they think nothing of it!
They take it completely for granted!
And they looked down on me!
They did not think me fit even to pick up their garbage!
But it will happen here. I will make it happen here. Believe me,
brother.

MUKHERJEE. Must I? I want to eat.

RHODES. Believe me first.

MUKHERJEE. Very well. I believe you. May I eat?
Women! Bring us food!

TWO. While the men talked

FOUR. The women had worked

TWO. And so they brought in food.

MUKHERJEE. Times have changed. Customs have degenerated.
When I was a boy my father was known as the father of the
village.
And the village was a family. A happy family. With our father
at the head of it.
And it was understood in those days. The village needed a
father.
As it still does. For the village still needs its father.
Now such things are forgotten. But then it was known.
Then it was understood. It was never questioned.
And the people trusted their father. They showed him respect.
For his shoulders were broad enough for all of their cares.
Everyone trusted him. Everyone greeted him.

And when the women served him food they served him with
joy. And with respect.
They were not surly. They did not give him slops!

SITA. We have served you. Isn't that enough?

MUKHERJEE. No Sita it is not enough!
There is an order in the world, Sita.
An order established by God.
My brother laughs. He thinks me old fashioned.
But I tell you there is an order
And at the heart of that order
Is the trust between men and women.
And if that trust is destroyed
Then the world falls to pieces.
There is a story in Shakespeare –

RHODES. Shakespeare!

SITA. I do not know Shakespeare.

MUKHERJEE. A writer of dramas, Sita. An English writer of
dramas.

RHODES. American.

MUKHERJEE. Pardon me, brother.

RHODES. He is American, brother. An American writer of
dramas.

MUKHERJEE. Forgive me, brother, but he is English. I know it
for a fact.

RHODES. Perhaps he was English once, brother, but now
England is finished. He is American.

MUKHERJEE. These are details, brother. They do not effect the
story!

RHODES. Listen to the story, Sita. The wise story from America.

MUKHERJEE. The story, Sita, of a woman who would obey
nobody.

RHODES. A beautiful woman, Sita. Very beautiful.

MUKHERJEE. But disobedient. A woman who listened to
nobody. A woman who would not obey. Not her father not her
sister not any man who tried to woo her. All were in terror of
her. Until her husband made her obey. He dragged her

through the mud and he whipped her and he denied her food. Then she obeyed. And she respected him for it. And respect, Sita, grew to love.
And then, Sita, order was restored. For she came to understand, Sita, something you do not seem to understand: that a proper relationship between man and woman is at the base of all things. The proper basis of all things. Think of it, Sita. Think of it.

RHODES. A beautiful story, Sita.

SITA. I do not think so.

MUKHERJEE. A very great man, Shakespeare. A wise man. Listen to his words, Sita. Or it will be the worse for you.

RHODES. Have you listened, Sita?

SITA. I have heard.

MUKHERJEE. You have heard with your ears but you have not listened with your heart.
Listen with your heart, Sita, I beg you.
Listen with your heart and give us peace.
You do not belong here, Sita.
When you came here you were in trouble and we took pity on you. We let you in.
And you have repaid us with nothing but trouble.
And we want peace. Peace in our village.
Peace in our world.
For the village is our world, and our world is this village.
It is the only world we have.
Now bring us tea.

Exit SITA.

RHODES. A woman of spirit.

MUKHERJEE. Father would have had her whipped.

RHODES. Father's dead, brother.

MUKHERJEE. We are the poorer for it.

RHODES. And so is your world. Dead and gone forever.

MUKHERJEE. I won't believe that. I will hang on as long as I can.
You laugh at me for being old fashioned, but wasn't life better then? Didn't it make more sense?

SITA *brings in tea.*

MUKHERJEE. In those days this was a great house. With glass in the windows and tiles on the walls. And our name on a plate by the door. And behind the house, quarters for animals and servants. Stables. We had a stable at the back for elephants! The whole village was ours then.
And the tea was hot! It was fit to drink!
Sita why is the tea cold?
Surely it is not too much to ask!
Civilisation, Sita, depends upon a supply of hot tea! Can you not understand!

RHODES. What became of the stove?

MUKHERJEE. What stove?

RHODES. The kerosene stove I brought the last time.

MUKHERJEE. I don't know. I don't concern myself with stoves!

SITA. It does not work.

RHODES. It worked when I left it.

SITA. It was a cheap stove.

RHODES. It was not cheap. It was a quality item. Woolworths! Fetch it!

Exit SITA.

RHODES. Brother I will deal with her.
I will deal with her and you will have peace in your home.
Light in your village and peace in your home.
I will tame her. I will make her see reason.
Leave it to me. Watch.

Enter SITA.

RHODES. Now Sita. Attend to me.

SITA. I attend you.

RHODES. Why does it not work?

MUKHERJEE. I expect she broke it. Being ignorant.

RHODES. Let me see.
There is no kerosene.
Brother did you not think to send for kerosene?

MUKHERJEE. It's no concern of mine.

RHODES. Where is your husband?

SITA. Washing.

RHODES. Send for him.

THREE. And so the poor man came.

 THREE *becomes* MUNTU.

MUNTU. Yes master. What do you wish master?

RHODES. We need kerosene. You will get it.

MUNTU. From where?

RHODES. From the town, of course. Where else?

MUNTU. How am I to wash the clothes?

RHODES. That is your affair.

MUKHERJEE. But I want them tomorrow!

RHODES. And they will be ready tomorrow. Or there will be
   trouble.

MUNTU. It cannot be done.

SITA. Muntu, go. I will wash the clothes.

RHODES. You hear that Muntu? Brother did you hear? The
   taming has begun! Congratulate me!

MUKHERJEE. I congratulate you.

RHODES. Sita can wash my clothes also. They are stained with
   the dust of the city. Muntu! You have not gone.

MUNTU. I have no money.

RHODES. The shopkeeper is a friend of mine. Explain. You will
   not have to pay.

MUNTU. The town is far away.

RHODES. The run will strengthen you.
   Now go.

SITA. Muntu. Go to the town. Take your chance.

THREE. And the poor man went.

FOUR. And the old woman dozed in the sun.

ONE. The landlord also slept.
   He was tired.

THREE. And Muntu ran to the town.

TWO. And the woman washed.

FIVE. And the brother lusted after her.

FOUR. And Kali said:

FOUR *becomes* KALI.

KALI. Once upon a time a long long time ago,
Before there were cities or aeroplanes or cars, everyone all
lived together.
By a great big river on a plain.

It stank. There were flies and dust and nothing ever happened.
But wives obeyed their husbands.
There was order in the world.
They bickered in the kitchens while the men drew patterns in
the dust.

One day someone drew a tower.
And another said "Let's build that. The women will make us
bricks."

And so they did. And the women baked the bricks.
And there they were. Baking bricks.
More and more fucking bricks.
All of them together.
All the women, sweating under the hot sun.
And they went on baking: they baked more and more and
more.

And the men kept building.
And the tower grew and grew.
That's all it did. Just grew.
It wasn't any use.
It wasn't any use to man nor beast.

And then a man said: "My brick has touched the sky" and
another said, "No! Mine has!"
And a third said: "Your bricks couldn't. They're all too soft."

And all at once they started shouting.

And the tower was about as big as a fifteenth part of my small
toenail,
And I said "You eejits. You fucking eejits."

So there they were. Imagine them!
They were all shouting and fighting over bits of string

And some of them were throwing down their bricks
To see how hard or soft they were.

The men never finished their high tower.
They were all shouting far too loud,
And anyway, they couldn't understand a word.

Babel, it was. Sheer babel.

And soon the fields were burning.

And do you know why it happened?
Because the women all obeyed their men!
The first stupidity. Original sin.

The triumph of the masculine mind.

THREE. And the poor man was still running to the town.

ONE. And the landlord still sleeping in his bed.

TWO. And the woman still washing the clothes.

FIVE. And the brother still lusting after her.

FIVE *becomes* RHODES.

RHODES. Her clothing was wet
Underneath her dress
I could trace the lines of her body.
Sita! Speak to me. Speak to me, Sita!
You think I hate you. But I do not hate you.
I respect you, Sita. I admire you.

SITA *says nothing*.

RHODES. Angry. Every time I come.
You're always angry.
To be angry does not become you, Sita.
Why are you so angry?

SITA. I am angry because I am poor.

RHODES. I too am poor. But I am not angry.

SITA. You are not poor.

RHODES. I started with nothing! Nothing at all! My brother was
given everything! Simply because he was born twenty minutes
sooner than me! That is all! But I am not angry. I have no time
to be angry. He has the time. The time to sit and read his
books. The time to sit and dream while the world falls to pieces

around him. He is so English, my brother. So very English. But I cannot afford to be English. I must work. Work for the good of the village.

SITA. Which is why you stole our land.

RHODES. It was a worthless piece of land! Why should we steal it? And how could we steal it when it was always ours? The thought of losing it distressed my brother. He is so sentimental! So I spoke to your husband and he agreed to give it back. I did not steal it.

SITA. You tricked him.

RHODES. I did not trick him.

SITA. You made him drunk.

RHODES. He was desperate to give me the land.
The land was far too big for him.
He is a tiny man. Weak in body.
Tiny in spirit. You are too strong for him.
He is so weak. So pathetically weak.
He has always been weak.
When he was a boy, Sita, we always used to make him carry stones. To see how long before he dropped them. It was never long. He simply hadn't the strength.

ONE. Muntu!

THREE *cowers down as the boy* MUNTU. *The others circle round.*

TWO. Little Muntu!

FOUR. Teeny Muntu!

FIVE. How high can you piss?
Higher than this?

TWO. Or this?

FOUR. Or this?

MUNTU *tries. A feeble effort. Everyone laughs.*

ONE. Muntu's lost his belt.

FIVE. Poor Muntu. Shall we help him find it?

They torment him by throwing it from one to the other.

MUNTU. I hate you! I hate you all!

ONE. He hates us!

FIVE. We're terrified!

> MUNTU *attacks* FIVE *and is easily overpowered. The others leave him crying.*

RHODES. He could never fight! He couldn't begin to fight!
It was amusing.

SITA. I do not find it amusing.

RHODES. Women have no sense of humour.
It's a well known fact.
And the strong have always preyed upon the weak.
It is the way of the world.
I am not weak, Sita. Because I made myself strong.
I was born weak.
They say my brother crushed me in the womb.
I was born so small and weak they say I almost died.
But I did not die, Sita.
I conquered myself and I grew strong.
My mother called me Manju. You laugh. Manju. A woman's
name. Meaning grace. I could not live with that name. So I
renounced it. I called myself Rhodes. Have you heard of
Rhodes, Sita? Cecil Rhodes? You do not know him, Sita. But I
know him. I read him in a book. A history book. My brother is
not the only one to read books! Cecil Rhodes. A great man. A
giant. A man who possessed nothing on the day he was born
but who when he was dying could be carried up a mountain
and know that everything he saw was his. A man who stopped
at nothing. Who found a continent in darkness and raised it to
the light.
For a man can do that. A single man. Believe me.
And I will do it, Sita. Not for the continent, but at least for the
village.
You think I am a bad man. But I am not a bad man.
I work for the good of the village.
You don't believe me.

SITA. No.

RHODES. You should believe me.

SITA. You're all talk. I can see through you.
All this talk of electricity. It's just a story!
You think you can get round us because we are poor.
You think you can deceive us because we're simple.
Well you can't get round me.
Don't think you can ever get round me.

RHODES. I am not a liar! I will bring light to this village!
And you will see! Tomorrow you will see!
I will do more for your village than your husband ever could.
He is too weak. Too stupid.
Did you see how I made him run?
Made him run for the kerosene?
He ran like a lamb. Like a lamb to the slaughter.
The shopkeeper will not give him kerosene!
But he let himself be fooled!
He will drag you down. Believe me.
You deserve better. Much better, Sita.
You are the only worthwhile thing. The only good thing in this village.
The only thing of value. The only thing of worth.
Believe me.
Why else do you think I come? To talk to my brother? To talk to my fat stupid brother who does nothing but sleep!
I come to see you. No one but you.
Sita in every town I visit, every village, there are women after me. Beautiful women.
But to me they are nothing.
Nothing compared to you.
Sita I have been to America.
Where the streets are full of beautiful women who hardly wear anything at all!
But they are hags compared to you.
My brother talks of light.
He talks of bringing light to the village when the light is there Right in front of his eyes.
For you are the light.
The light of the village.
The light of the village and washing my clothes. I am honoured.
Don't do that!
Don't do that to my clothes!
How can you do this?
How can you ignore me?
How can you remain so cold?
How can you turn me away?
Don't you hear what I'm saying?
Don't you understand?
Leave your husband and come to me!

SITA. No.

RHODES. Come to the city. Come to the city with me.

You're too good for this village.
Come Sita. Come. You left your last husband.

SITA. It's a lie.

RHODES. Oh Sita. Don't play the prude with me. Don't play the hypocrite.

SITA. I will not leave my husband.

RHODES. Then stay with him. You can still come to me.
I am not like my brother. I am not stuck in the past.
I am a modern man. And we can be modern in these matters, Sita. We can talk about them openly. We can leave the dark ages behind.
You are a woman, Sita. You have needs.
Needs he can't satisfy. Him so weak.
Come to me and I will satisfy. You will have your fill of me.
Be practical, Sita. Be wise.
The debt will be cleared, Sita, and you will be free.

SITA. No.

RHODES. You can cultivate the land.

SITA. No.

RHODES. I will give you a child.

SITA. No!

RHODES. He can't do that. He'll never give you one. You know that.

Silence.

Yes. That, Sita. You know that.
And you will change your mind.
He is weak, Sita. Remember that.

SITA. He is kind!

RHODES. Kindness is not everything.

SITA. Kindness is all we have.

RHODES. There is no kindness in the world.

SITA. There has to be. Or none of us would be here. None of us. We would all be dead.
We owe our lives to kindness.

RHODES. Only the weak.

SITA. I was hungry and he let me in. You never let me in.
   None of you let me in.
   You stayed in your houses and you locked the door.
   He let me in. Muntu. The man you all despise for being weak!
   He was not afraid.
   He fed me. Fed me with his hands!
   He went hungry to give me food!
   And then he told me stories to try to make me laugh.
   He's worth ten of you.

RHODES. No Sita. He is weak. Remember that.
   He is weak and I am strong.

SITA. If you're that strong, then wash your clothes.

FIVE. And she gave him his sodden clothes and walked away.

RHODES. You bitch! You'll regret this!
   You'll pay for this!

ONE. And the landlord slept.

THREE. And the poor man ran back to the village.

SITA. Did you hear that?
   Did you hear that?

MEENA. I heard.

SITA (mimics RHODES). "Come to me and I will satisfy!"
   Him! I'd rather kiss a toad!

MEENA. You should.

SITA. What?

MEENA. Go to him. Apologise.

SITA. Apologise?

MEENA. He'll make you pay.

SITA. He'll be gone tomorrow!

MEENA. He'll come back.

SITA. I don't care.

MEENA. He'd be better than Muntu. He'd be strong.

SITA. My last husband was strong.
   Strong as an ox, they said, and a wealthy man.
   They said I was lucky to have him.

And I believed them. I thought so too.
Until the doors closed behind us on our wedding night. Then I
knew better.
He never said a kind word, or a gentle one,
He spoke to me as if I did not exist. As if I were a thing.
In the end he turned me out.
He found another wife. A better one, he said.
He said I was a witch. I'd given him a girl.
I've had enough of strength.

MEENA. I never knew.

SITA. They turned me away. My own village!
Turned me away. I walked for days.
Weeks. I carried my child.
She cried and cried.
I had to close my heart
Or she would have torn it to pieces.
I closed my heart. I turned it into stone.
She was silent at the end
So small so shrunken and so old
With enormous empty hollow eyes.

We buried her. Muntu and I.
Buried her under the tree.

But she had the right!
She had the right to be in the world!

FOUR. And Kali said:

ONE *becomes* KALI.

KALI 1. Don't think there ever was a paradise.
Don't believe any stories of a happy past.

TWO *becomes* KALI.

KALI 2. Don't imagine a garden where the first people walked.

THREE *becomes* KALI.

KALI 3. A forbidden garden
A garden of earthly delights
A garden you are barred from
And can never enter again.

FOUR *becomes* KALI.

KALI 4. The earth was never like a garden.
It was too wild.

FIVE *becomes* KALI.

KALI 5. There were no little lawns
Or flower beds.

KALI 1. It was a forest
Wilder than any forest in your wildest dreams.

KALI 2. Wilder than the forests now
The pale echo of the early forests,

KALI 3. The forests that you now destroy.

KALI 4. And there you took your pleasure.

KALI 5. By rivers of flowing water,

KALI 1. Under the shelter of the giant trees.

KALI 4. And you can go back there when you want
You can walk naked hand in hand
You can kiss and touch
And nothing stops you.
If there is a door
You are the ones who hold the key.

ONE. And Muntu was still running back to the village.

TWO. He had good news.

FOUR. And Kali hovered over him and touched his thigh

TWO. And he began to dream

MUNTU. Of spitting in his master's face
Of kicking in his brother's
Of wearing great big boots
And trampling them both into the mud forever!
Of making love to Sita for hours and hours.

TWO. And the woman was picking up the washing with her
weary back
And fixing it on the hedge to dry

ONE. And it wasn't properly clean!

THREE. And Muntu came back and said:

MUNTU. Sita. Sita! I saw the lawyer!
He's going to help us!

SITA. What?

MUNTU. I saw the lawyer! When I was in town!
    At first I couldn't understand. But then I knew! That's why
    you did the washing!
    That's why you told me to go.
    I saw that when I got to the shop.
    The shopkeeper wouldn't give me kerosene. He laughed in my
    face.

SITA. You were tricked!

MUNTU. Tricked again! I knew it!
    They think I'm nothing, Sita!
    Worth less than an umbrella!
    An American umbrella!
    I was so angry! I ran to the lawyer's.
    He was easy to find. Everyone knows him. Everyone wants to
    see him. I hardly dared go on. But I thought of you. And then
    went on. You gave me courage.
    The door was guarded. There were men with guns. I told them
    who I was, I said I am from this village. And they did not
    laugh at me. They let me in!
    And the room was full of people.
    People standing. People sitting.
    People lying on the ground.
    There was a man with no hand
    A woman with no eyes
    Children with suppurating sores.
    Angry men. Tired men. Men sunk in the deepest despair. A
    man so thin and shrivelled he looked as if you could blow him
    away.
    And they looked as if they had been waiting for days.
    And then he came.

    ONE *becomes the* LAWYER.

LAWYER. Muntu. It is Muntu!
    Don't you recognise me?

MUNTU. You have changed.

LAWYER. But I know you. I have been waiting, waiting for you
    to come.
    And you are welcome. Come in. Come!
    Have tea!

MUNTU. You give me tea! A lawyer and you give me tea!

LAWYER. You gave me more than tea! You gave me light!
Light in a dark time.
Muntu. Have you forgotten? You helped me. You helped me
study.

MUNTU. I did nothing. I could never help you. It was all too
hard for me.

LAWYER. I had nowhere to study and you found me space.
Beside the cows, remember? Beside the landlord's cows. And
you held the light.

MUNTU. It was nothing that I did, nothing at all.

LAWYER. Without you I would have died. I could not work in
the fields, I could not study, I was good for nothing but death.
And you saved me.
I have been waiting. I told the guards at the door to admit
anyone from our village.
Anyone who comes.
And at last you have come!
But tell me. How can I serve you?

MUNTU. And I told him.

LAWYER I remember that will. The old partner drew it up. We
were amazed.
Peasants are not often given land.
But listen Muntu: the will still stands.
They are bound by its terms.
The paper they tricked you into signing counts for nothing.
You are not bound by it.
Dig the ground. Plant seeds.
If they cause trouble come back to me.
You showed me kindness, Muntu.
I will not forget.

MUNTU. A good man. A good man, Sita, but so tired.
So tired and grey.

SITA. Shall we do it?
Shall we dig the ground?

MUNTU. Shall we?

MEENA. No. Don't touch the land.
Don't trust the lawyer.
The lawyer's very far away.
And I know this village.

The brothers will destroy you
And no one will lift a finger to help.

SITA. But they don't care about the land.
The brother told me.

MEENA. Don't believe him. I know this village.
This is where I was born.
When I was a child I knew it all.
I knew each blade of grass. The sky was my own, and all the
birds in it. And all the trees had faces. Some were good, some
bad. The good ones I knew to be my friends.
Or thought I knew.
There was so much I did not understand. I couldn't
understand the sickness. I saw my mother shivering in the
noonday heat and asked her, mother, mother, why are you
so cold?
She never answered.
And I did not, ever, understand.
Debt I did not understand. And I was sold to pay it. Sold to
pay my parent's debt.
Sold to a man in the city!
And in the city this is what I learnt:
That you have to fight.
Fight for every inch of pavement, every corner of a room.
And there is no family. There is no home.
There are no ties of gratitude or blood.
The stronger wins. The weaker dies.
And if you faint they'll pass you by. As if you were a stone!
I dreamt of coming back. I used to think the village was a
better place.
But there is no safety in the village.
I was a fool.
A fool to remember the trees and all the different blades of
grass.
And a kind of flower that used to grow round here.
A small one. White. And with a yellow stem.
I remembered it all the years of the city.
I never forgot.
A fool. A fool to remember!
I saved and I saved because I wanted to come back. And I
wanted my children to see it.
And I did come back. And no one knew me.
My children left me.
I couldn't find the flower.
It doesn't seem to grow here any more.

ONE. And the old woman was wise.

FIVE. They should have listened.

ONE. But they did not.

FIVE. And they had to pay.

SITA. She's very old.

MUNTU. Very afraid.

SITA. I'm sure she's wrong.
    Muntu. We have to do it.

MUNTU. Let's do it.

SITA. Let's do it now.

MUNTU. Now?

SITA. It's new year tomorrow.
    The day we should plant the seeds.

MUNTU. No one will see us.

SITA. Not now it's getting dark.

MUNTU. I'll steal a spade.

FOUR. So they tiptoed past the sunset to the patch of ground.

ONE. And began to dig the ground.

FOUR. The small useless patch of ground.

ONE. The worst land in the village.

FOUR. Because it was all they had.

ONE. All they would ever hope to have.

MUNTU. Are you afraid?

SITA. Yes.

MUNTU. So am I.
    What shall we do?

SITA. Do it anyway.

ONE. And so they dug.

FOUR. They dug in the gathering darkness.

ONE. And no one saw them or praised them or gave them medals.

FOUR. Because they wereni killing anyone or doing harm.

ONE. They were only planting seeds.

FOUR. They should have been planting mines.

ONE. They'd have been "Our brave boys".

FOUR. And they'd have made it on the news.

   SITA *and* MUNTU *are kissing*.

ONE. What happened instead was something else.

FOUR. A miracle.

ONE. Kali touched them and his manhood rose.

FOUR. And she opened like a flower.

SITA. He was strong, but he was not clumsy or fierce
   And suddenly everything was right
   I was not a block of wood
   I was not made of stone
   I was not a sanctuary or a holy place
   I was not a piece of fenced-in ground
   I wanted to love him and I found I could.

MUNTU. I can't explain. I can't explain a thing!

SITA. I lay on top with delight inside me.

MUNTU. Rocking to and fro!
   She was rocking to and fro!
   It was bliss . . .

SITA. I was playing my body
   My body was a song of pleasure.

MUNTU. The past was gone and the future too
   There was just now.

SITA. And now.

MUNTU. And now!

ONE. And there was no division.

FOUR. No fear.

MUNTU. I was she.

SITA. And I was he.

MUNTU. And she was me.

SITA. And me and he and he and me.

MUNTU. And it all went on for ever and ever.

FOUR *becomes* KALI.

KALI. It used to be so much easier to fuck.
You all just went and did it
Where you found it on the ground
And it didni matter who or what you were
Men with women, women with men.

ONE *becomes* KALI.

KALI 1. Men with men.

KALI 4. Women with women

KALI 1. Because you knew it didn't matter.

KALI 4. You knew that all that mattered was the love

KALI 1. Until you built the tower.

KALI 4. Till you discovered warfare
And then discovered shame.

KALI 1. And then it all got codified

KALI 4. By yon grey fucker. Him with the beard.
Him and his tablets of stone.

TWO. Meanwhile the lovers just went on and on

THREE. Till they were tired

FOUR. And fell asleep,

ONE. Happy in the open air

TWO. Open and free. Open and free!

FOUR. While the landlord tossed on his lonely bed.

ONE. Pity the rich! Pity the lonely rich!

THREE. And Muntu had a happy dream.

KALI. Muntu! Muntu!

MUNTU. What is it?

KALI. Something for you.

MUNTU. A present?

KALI. Yes. A present. Your heart's desire.

MUNTU. For me?

KALI. For you.

MUNTU. But who are you?

KALI. Don't question the giver. Take the gift.

MUNTU. It's a baby!

KALI. Of course it's a baby.

MUNTU. He's beautiful.

KALI. She, Muntu.

MUNTU. Sorry.

KALI. She is beautiful.

MUNTU. How can you give her to me?

KALI. Because she's mine.

MINTU. How can a mother give away her child?

KALI. Because I made her.

MUNTU. Mother Kali . . . forgive . . . I didn't know . . .

KALI. Don't worship me! You'll wake the baby!

MUNTU. Sorry.

KALI. See Muntu, a child is just a tiny thing
  It only takes a moment to make.
  Children are easy to create.
  Think, Muntu: a child is just a thing of bones and flesh and
  blood. A simple thing, Muntu.
  Filled with a little air.
  And so common, Muntu.
  Common as dirt.
  It's loving them that's difficult.
  So take her Muntu. Love her. Love her well.

  KALI *goes*.

MUNTU. Sita. Sita look!

SITA. What is it?

MUNTU. A child! We've been given a child.
  Look, Sita, take her.
  A girl. A little girl.

She'll grow up beautiful and strong.
She'll go to school.
She won't suffer from ignorance the way we have.
She won't be poor. She won't be in debt.
She won't work and work for nothing.
She'll become a lawyer.
She'll fight for justice! She will fight the rich!
What's wrong?

SITA *has unravelled the empty bundle.*

SITA. Look.

MUNTU. But it was a child!
   I swore I saw a child!

SITA. You were dreaming.
   Your baby's just a piece of cloth. A rag.

MUNTU. How could I dream such a thing?

SITA. I'm going home. It's cold.

   Exit SITA. MUNTU *is alone.*

MUNTU. But where did the cloth come from?
   It isn't ours!
   And we dug the ground. That was no dream!
   And then we made love. That was no dream!
   And then . . . What if it was a dream?
   Sita! Where have you gone?
   What if it was just a dream?
   I held my child!
   I won't forget. I won't, I won't.
   I won't forget!

ACT TWO

TWO. And then when morning came

MUNTU. Muntu had forgotten everything.

ONE. And when the landlord woke . . .

MUKHERJEE. I saw my clothes.
  Muntu! Muntu! MUNTU!

MUNTU. Yes master.

MUKHERJEE. Do you call this clean?

MUNTU. Yes master.

MUKHERJEE. Then you are ignorant, Muntu.
  Ignorant and dirty.

MUNTU. I did my best.

MUKHERJEE. It wasn't good enough.

MUNTU. My wife had to finish the clothes.

MUKHERJEE. So you blame your wife.

MUNTU. I had to go for kerosene!

MUKHERJEE. And did you get some?

MUNTU. The shopkeeper wouldn't give me any.

MUKHERJEE. Muntu you have failed me.

MUNTU. Yes master.

MUKHERJEE. Muntu you are not attending.

MUNTU. No master.

MUKHERJEE. Why not?

MUNTU. I've forgotten something.

MUKHERJEE. What?

MUNTU. I can't remember.

MUKHERJEE. Out of my sight! Go!

I'll have to dress myself!
In second rate clothes!

TWO. When Sita woke she felt both happy and afraid.
Something was happening. For good or ill.
Something was happening at last.
The years of drudgery were over.

FIVE. When the brother woke

RHODES. I completed my preparations,
I unpacked my bulbs,
I unrolled my wires,
But it was no use.
I thought of Sita.
I want to fuck Sita!

FOUR. When Meena woke

MEENA. I woke up sighing.
I'd been in such a happy place,
Where my limbs didn't creak
And I was myself again.

RHODES. A man should not need a woman.
A man should not need a woman at all.
Even Rhodes was led astray by a woman.
Rhodes himself. Cecil Rhodes! By a countess.
A German countess. A beautiful German countess!
She lured him. Lured him into ruin and disgrace.
I'll work. I'll work!
I have a job to do. A vital task!
Work that needs all my concentration. All my strength!
Fittings to fit. Connections to make. Dangerous work!
And all I can think of are Sita's breasts.
The space between Sita's breasts. The magical place. The
blissful space. I'll work. I'll work!
And Sita. Sita walking. Sita smiling. If she'd only smile. If she'd
only smile at me!

SITA *walks by. She carries water.*

Sita! Don't ignore me!
I'm doing this for you!
Sita I'm about to risk my life!
Sita this is dangerous. Far more dangerous than anything the
heroes used to do. Than anything Rama ever did. Sita.
Sita and Rama.

I'll be your Rama, Sita! Better than Rama!
Rama just fought demons. But there were no demons ever as
strong as this! No demons ever had the power of electricity.

And Rama never tamed his demons. Rama never made them
work for him. He never used them to transform the world. As
I will Sita. As I will right now!
Sita look at me!
Sita there's a man on the city streets
A man lying on the filth of the city streets
A helpless man. A man without arms!
A man with nothing but two tiny useless stumps!
A man who climbed up to a cable, Sita,
As I am doing now,
A man climbing up a cable to do his people good.
The current caught him and burnt off his arms.
Burnt them to cinders! He fell to the ground and he broke his
back!
And so he lies on the pavement and begs for pennies from the
passers by!
And it could happen to me, Sita. It could happen to me!
If I were a cripple Sita would you look after me?
Would you wipe the dust from my forehead and the flies from
my lips?
Would you feed me with your fingers and dribble water in my
mouth?
Think of it, Sita. What degradation for a man!
What humiliation!
But I would gladly suffer it for you!
Anything would be better than have you ignore me!
Sita! I'm about to do it!
I'm about to connect the wires!
I'm doing it, Sita! I'm doing it now!

SITA. And nothing happens.
Nothing was ever going to happen.
You fraud!

RHODES. Frigid bitch! You'll see! You'll see what I'll do for you!

MUKHERJEE. This is a sad day. A sad day for me. This day
which used to be the finest day in the whole of the year. When
everyone decorated their houses and wore their finest clothes
and the musicians played from morning to night. And
everyone danced and threw coloured water and everyone's
cares were forgotten. We were all one, on that day. All one. All
one happy village. Meena! You'll remember!

MEENA. No.

MUKHERJEE. You're too old.

MEENA. I remember the chair.

MUKHERJEE. What chair?

MEENA. The chair the old man sat in. Your father.

MUKHERJEE. His brown leather chair. A Parker-Knoll. From England.

MEENA. He'd sit on it like a throne. He'd have it placed under the village tree, and come out and sit on it on Fridays to take his rent. And we'd all line up and hand over our piles of tattered notes. All the people in the village. And before we gave it him we always had to bow. There'd be a bailiff right beside him with the ledger book.

MUKHERJEE. Old Rajiv. A kind man.

MEENA. Skinflint.

MUKHERJEE. He used to give me sweets.

MEENA. And if you couldn't pay in cash he'd make you pay in kind. When things got bad he'd take your chickens or your goats. There was always someone crying. Because you'd be lost without your beasts. Your children would go hungry: and in the end he'd turn you out.

MUKHERJEE. That wasn't how it was. That was the weekly ceremony. For giving thanks. It wasn't about rent at all. And there was music. There was always music.

MEENA. There was always the squealing of a stuck pig. He liked his bit of pork.

MUKHERJEE. He was hard, but just.

MEENA. He was like a kind of god. A stern god. A stern and angry god. He was so big! He swallowed up the village. He ate too much. Towards the end he couldn't walk. They had to carry him about. And then he got too big for that. They had to lift him up onto a cart. They had to use a crane!

MUKHERJEE. He had dignity.

MEENA. He looked so stupid. Hanging there. His legs dangling. Your brother once got punished because he saw him and he smiled. They whipped him for showing disrespect. Manju he was then. How he cried.

MUKHERJEE. Meena you remember wrong.

MEENA. No. I remember.

MUKHERJEE. We have to remember. We have to remember right. If we lose the past, we lose the present. If we lose the present, then we lose the future too. We lose everything. We must remember. We mustn't forget. But the music. Meena. You remember the music.

MEENA. There used to be an old man with a battered drum.

MUKHERJEE. No you don't remember well. There were streets of musicians. Whole quarters of musicians. And music would be with us every minute of our lives. Music at every birth. At every coming of age. At every wedding. Every funeral. Each festival. Each day was the occasion for a song.
But now the shops of the musicians are shuttered and the music makers have all gone.

TWO. And while the landlord was remembering the past

RHODES. His brother was building the future.

TWO. Stringing up a little row of bulbs.

FOUR. To make the village like Chicago.

TWO. And was the village like Chicago?

RHODES. But it's a start! At least I've made a start!
At least I'm trying!
And we can't go on like this.
Scratching a living from the soil
Toiling away with broken tools
Celebrating our pathetic little festivals
That don't mean a thing to anyone any more!
It's all the past,
It's all got to be swept away.
Everything will change!
And this is what will make it change!

He holds up a light bulb.

And none of you understand. None of you care and none of you understand. But I'm doing it for you! Can't you see that, at least? I'm doing it for you!

KALI. Once there was a man who had a vision come from God. Not from me. From God. And this is true.
And God came to the man and said "Build me a boat". And the

man said "O my God" and God said "What's wrong?" and the
man said "God I'm a dairy farmer. I don't know a thing about
building boats." And God didn't listen. He never does.
He just said "Listen son you just have to build this boat. Don't
you argue with me.
Just build it. And I want it this big. In cubits."
And the man said "Cubits? We use yards".
And God created measuring tape and then he said "See you.
Just you build this bloody boat. No arguing. Right? And see
yon tree? I'll knock it down for you to give you a start".
And so he did. Crash! And then he went.
And the man started building. And his cows mooed and his
children cried and his wife just yelled at him all the day.
And he said "Don't you blame me. Blame God".
And he went on building. He enjoyed it. He had his shed. And
he just worked away, stopping now and then to have his wee bit
smoke.
And then it was finished and he felt right proud. There was
only one thing wrong:
No water.
It was a dry country.
And they were miles away from the sea.
Everybody laughed at him.
But then the water started rising. A miracle!
Bit by bit at first, and then a foot a day.
And everything began to disappear. Everything he'd ever
known or loved or cared for.
And all the neighbours ran away.
They told him he had to leave as well.
But he took no heed of them. He said "We've got our boat"
and he felt right proud.
He got everyone together, his wife, his children, and all his
beasts.
And then he put them in his boat.
But he had a problem. There wasn't room for all of them and
for their food. The boat just wasn't big enough. Cubits wereni
big those days. So he called out "God! God!" he shouted
"Where are you bastard? Can you no hear me? God!"
But God didni hear him. God had buggered off.
So they all got in. They had to.
And the water rose and rose.
And they drifted on a grey and featureless sea.
Everything had gone. The house they had built, the shed
where they kept the cows. The neighbour's house and the

muddy pond the children used to splash in. The square in the
village where the elders met. The school. The big house and
the temple. All of it had gone. Everything that made their
world.
They drifted, in the open, under the pitiless sky.
But they hadni far to go.
Just to the dam's high wall.
The dam the world bank built for electricity.

RHODES. Forget the past. All of you! Forget the past!
Come and see the future.
Look!

MUKHERJEE. Is this the future?

RHODES. What else could it be!
What do you think? All of you! What do you think!

MUKHERJEE. Gaudy.

RHODES. Is that all you can say?

MUKHERJEE. Garish.

RHODES. Garish!

MUKHERJEE. That is, I think, the most appropriate word.

RHODES. How about amazing? Astonishing? Extraordinary? A
remarkable achievement?

MUKHERJEE. You've simply strung up some coloured bulbs. I
refuse to be impressed.

RHODES. Wait till I turn the power on.

MUKHERJEE. I will wait.

RHODES. There!
Isn't it wonderful?

MUDKHERJEE. No.

RHODES. Brother!

MUKHERJEE. It hardly shows.

RHODES. That's because it's daylight! Wait till night!

MUKHERJEE. Brother if this is the modern age, then you can
keep it.

RHODES. My brother does not like the modern age.
Simply because he does not understand it.

Even in this bulb, this tiny manifestation of power,
There is a force beyond your wildest dreams.
Were one of you, with your puny force, to try to keep this bulb
alight you would have to run at full stretch for hour after hour.
But you do not have to run, or work or move
The power will be there at your disposal
There whenever you want or need it
You won't have to spend hours kneading cow dung for the fuel
for your pitiful fires.
You won't have to spend hours grinding your spices or your
corn.
You won't have to wash clothes in this filthy pond!
A machine will do it for you.

MEENA. We'll lose our jobs.

RHODES. Then we'll find you different work. Better work.

MEENA. Work's all the same.

RHODES. No Meena. Work is not all the same. There is
drudgery, Meena, and there is labour. There is subsistence,
Meena, and there are wages. Real wages. Money in your
pocket.
An end to debt. Think about it.
You could own your house.
You could own a piece of land.
And more than that. You could buy furniture. A bed. You
could buy a bed! And carpets for the floor. You'll have lights in
the house.
There'll be no more cowering in the dark after the sun's gone
down.
All this and more will be yours.
At a reasonable price.
On most reasonable terms.

MUKHERJEE. Brother have you no shame?

RHODES. Why should I be ashamed?

MUKHERJEE. This is the festival!
I should speak first!
As your elder brother!

RHODES. Speak then brother. We are agog.

FOUR. And the crowd all sighed and settled down.

THREE. Except for Muntu.

MUNTU. Sita.

SITA. What?

MUNTU. What will happen?

SITA. What will happen when?

MUNTU. When they find out we've dug the land?

SITA. Perhaps they won't find out.

MUNTU. But they will!

SITA. Why?

MUNTU. Because it's today! Everyone dances round the village!

SITA. So what can we do?

MUNTU. I don't know.

SITA. What's done is done.

MUNTU. Yes.

SITA. We have to stand our ground.

MUNTU. Yes.

SITA. Why should they care?

MUNTU. They will. I know they will.

SITA. Muntu, an old year is ending. An old time. Something new
will begin.

MUNTU. Will it?

SITA. Yes. Don't be afraid. Last night you weren't afraid.

MUNTU. That was last night.

SITA. There's no sense in being afraid.

MUNTU. It makes perfect sense to me.

FOUR. Meanwhile!
The landlord stood lost in thought.

ONE. He was nervous.

FOUR. And the crowd began to shuffle their feet.

RHODES. Begin, brother! Begin!

MUKHERJEE. Friends! There was a happier time when my
father stood

Where I am standing now.
There was a time when he would be speaking to a crowd,
When the whole village stopped to hear his words.
Weeks would be spent in fevered preparation,
In joyful anticipation of this sacred moment.
The moment of his speech. Of this feast.
Not a feast for gluttons of the flesh
But for gluttons of the spirit of the spoken word.
There is a wisdom in the past, he would always say,
And we ignore it at our peril.
There is a wisdom in the ancient ordering of things
Between high and low
Between men and women
Between the master and the servant.
Each needs the other, and in the other
Each is most fulfilled.
Because happiness does not come from riches
Happiness does not come from a mad disordered scramble for
wealth.
Happiness comes from doing one's allotted task
And knowing one's place in the order of things.
At this festival it is the custom for each to make a wish.
And to call down the blessing of the Gods upon it.
In former times these were universal wishes:
Wishes we all could share and know to be our own.
The wish for prosperity in our seeding
And a fruitful harvest.
The wish for fertility in our fields,
Contentment in our hearts and minds.
Things are not so simple nowadays.
Something has shattered the old collectiveness.
All of us are splintered. Individuals alone.
But let us try to recapture the spirit of the past. Let us wish for
harmony and concord.
Wish that we may know our place
And be content in it.

RHODES. Have you finished brother?

MUKHERJEE. I think so. I think I put it rather well.

RHODES. Then that's for you!
Death to the past!

He drops a bomb of coloured water onto MUKHERJEE's *head.*

A pause. MUKHERJEE *tries to mop himself.*

MUKHERJEE. That was uncalled for.

RHODES. So was your speech.

MEENA. And that's for your father!

MUNTU. And that's for the past!

SITA. And that's for knowing your place!

They all drench him.

MUKHERJEE. But friends, what have I done?
What have I done to deserve this?

RHODES. It's the festival brother.
When we drench each other with coloured water.
When we celebrate our togetherness.
Have you forgotten?

MUKHERJEE. In that case, brother, that's for you!
Death to science!

He drenches RHODES. MUNTU *laughs.* RHODES *drenches*
MUNTU. MUNTU *laughs louder.* MUNTU *drenches* RHODES.
RHODES *drenches* SITA. *Etc. Etc. Everyone laughs. A wild moment.*

RHODES. Death to ignorance!

MUNTU. Death to wealth!

MUKHERJEE. Death to America!

RHODES. Death to Shakespeare!

MUNTU. Death to England!

RHODES. Death to culture!

MUKHERJEE. Death to women!

MEENA. Death to men!

MUNTU. Death to electricity!

SITA. Death to husbands!

MUNTU. Death to wives!

RHODES. Death to life!

MUKHERJEE. Death to diagrams!

RHODES. Death to books!

MEENA. Death to death!

ALL. LONG LIVE FREEDOM!

A wild dance. MUKHERJEE *suddenly stops dead.*

MUKHERJEE. Muntu! MUNTU!

The laughter dies.

MUNTU *approaches like a naughty child.*

MUKHERJEE. Hold out your hands.

MUNTU *holds out his hands.* MUKHERJEE *strikes them.*

MUKHERJEE. Someone has been digging the land, Muntu.
   My land. My father's land. My father's father's land. And the
   land of his father before him too!
   Someone is trying to steal this land, Muntu. Was it you?
   I don't want to believe it was you.
   After all we've done for you.
   All the work we've given you.
   I don't want to think you would betray us.
   Muntu. Say it wasn't you.
   Say it wasn't you and we'll forget all about it.

TWO. And all the village looked at him.

FOUR. And the poor man was afraid.

TWO. All his courage left him.

THREE. All his dreams and his desires.

MUKHERJEE. Muntu?

MUNTU. No master. I never touched the land.
   Why should I dig your land?
   Why should I dig it when it isn't mine?

SITA. It isn't theirs! It isn't!
   How could you betray us?

MUKHERJEE. And now we know. Now the criminals show
   themselves.
   Muntu, Muntu! How could you do this to me?
   We gave you everything!
   You try to steal back the land!
   The land kept sacred to my father's memory

MUNTU. He gave it to me.

MUKHERJEE. But you gave it back.

MUNTU. The lawyer said I could.

MUKHERJEE. You have seen a lawyer?
  So that's why you got no kerosene.
  Shame on you Muntu! Shame!
  Your parents went to see a lawyer too.
  Some disgraceful protest.
  They ate poisoned food and died.
  The food of their ingratitude.
  My father could have let you starve
  You were an orphan and we took you in!
  And my father had no reason to!
  He just did it out of kindness!

SITA. He wanted a servant he wouldn't have to pay!

RHODES. We know who the criminal is.
  Muntu. We know it wasn't you.
  Now redeem yourself.
  Tie her hands.

MUNTU. No.

RHODES. You see this Muntu? You see this knife?
  What shall it cut? Her eyes? Her nose?

SITA. No. No!

RHODES. Tie her Muntu or she will come to harm.
  Tie her. Tie her with the wire. The electric wire. This is the
  modern age.

SITA. Don't do it Muntu.

MUNTU. I have no choice.

RHODES. Quite right.

SITA. MUNTU!

RHODES. I'll shut your mouth.

  He kisses her. She spits at him.

RHODES. Now you spit Muntu. Spit on her. She has
  shamed you.
  Spit Muntu. Spit!

MUNTU. No.

RHODES. Spit. Spit. Spit!

  He beats MUNTU.

RHODES. You still haven't learnt to fight. Foolish.
  Now spit.

MUNTU *spits*.

MUNTU. Forgive me.

RHODES. Now brother.
  But my brother is afraid.
  My elder brother is afraid.

MUKHERJEE. I want no part in this.

RHODES. But you do brother. I know you do.
  You have dreamt of this.
  This is taming her, brother. The taming of the wild!
  And don't whine to me of culture.
  This is culture.

FOUR. And then they raped her in the village square.

RHODES. I rammed into her like she was a dog.

SITA. I screamed but did not scream enough
  I could never scream enough
  Not if I'd filled the sky with screaming
  Not if I'd filled the sky!

RHODES. She screamed for mercy but she wanted more
  More and more and more and more!

SITA. There was pain
  But there was worse than pain.

RHODES. Her beauty hurt me
  So I wanted to destroy it
  I wanted her to be an ugly thing
  I wanted her to be no more than dirt.

SITA. I wasn't a woman I was just a thing
  An ugly hole they poured their filth in.

RHODES. That's all they are in the end.
  All of them.
  Dirt.

SITA. I fought but did not fight enough
  Something in me told me to submit
  Something said it wouldn't hurt as much.

RHODES. She never gave me pleasure.
  She was dry. Arid. A frigid bitch.

SITA. What if we really fought
  What if we used our strength
  What if we really used our strength.

RHODES. She would keep making this ugly noise.
  It was distracting me.
  I stuffed her mouth with dirt.

FOUR. They'd tied the husband to a post
  Someone hit him if he looked away
  Or tried to close his eyes.

ONE. And then the landlord had his turn.

MUKHERJEE. It was regrettable,
  Painful for a man of culture
  But she needed a lesson.
  I did my duty.
  Or at least I tried.

FOUR. Everyone was watching.
  She just lay there, defeated in the dirt.

MUKHERJEE. Men are meant to dream of this,
  Of a woman's body lying there
  Open. Vulnerable. Exposed.
  Mine for the taking.
  I stand here and I'm filled with shame.
  But can't go back.
  Everyone is watching.

RHODES. My brother couldn't keep his prick up
  He was just pretending!

MUKHERJEE. Brother, for shame!

RHODES. You're the one. You're the one, brother,
  You're the one to be ashamed.

TWO. And the sun went down in the sky.

FOUR. Ants scurried along the ground.

TWO. Carrying the most enormous weights.

FOUR. And no one knew where they were going.

TWO. Bees sucked flowers.
  Spiders made their webs.

FOUR. Birds sang high in the sky.

TWO. And life went on.
  Life just went on!

ONE. The brothers left her in the dirt.

TWO. And boys came and pissed on her.

BOY. I was higher! I was higher than you!

ONE. It was the carnival.

TWO. And that was the coming of the light.
  That was how light came to the village.

MUKHERJEE. Muntu. Muntu I'm sorry.
  Muntu I didn't know.
  Muntu I didn't mean . . .

RHODES. Muntu, man to man, take my advice
  Get rid of her. You'll get no pleasure from her.
  She's coming Muntu.
  She's crawling after me.

  SITA *and* MUNTU *together a moment.*

SITA. Don't you touch me.
  Don't you ever touch me!

MUNTU. I shouldn't have let them touch you.
  I should have died.
  Why didn't I?
  Why didn't I die?

  Enter KALI.

MUNTU. Mother Kali
  Is this a punishment?

KALI. What for?

MUNTU. I forgot your dream.

KALI. Dinni be daft. Get some water.
  Get the old woman.
  Get organised.
  Muntu, I don't punish and I do not judge.
  People make punishments for themselves.
  Now stop moping. She needs you.
  She needs your help!

MUNTU. But what about the child?

KALI. What child?

MUNTU. You said we'd have a child.

KALI. You'll get your child.
　A child of blood.
　A child to overturn the world!
　My child! You've been chosen, Muntu.
　God knows why. And don't thank me. Go!

　Sita you cannot see me
　Sita you cannot hear me
　You cannot feel or touch me
　You're lost in a cold dark place where comfort never comes.
　But I am with you.
　And my heart bleeds. It bleeds for you.
　Listen, Sita. Listen in the dark.
　Don't listen to the men, Sita. Listen to me.
　They want you to think you're finished. Used up. Wrung dry.
　Chucked in the dung heap like a dirty rag. They're wrong.
　They want you to think that every part is full of dirt. Their
　dirt. That there's nowhere they have not defiled or soiled.
　They're wrong. They're very wrong.
　They want you to feel guilty. That you're to blame. That you
　deserve no better.
　How many women have they done it to?
　How many women, Sita? How many of us?
　The men in uniforms and business suits
　The men who make the laws
　And then tell us that we should be ashamed.
　For they will tell you that.
　They'll tell you that you had it coming
　That you asked for it
　That it's all that you deserve.
　Listen. Don't be ashamed. You've no cause to be ashamed. It
　wasn't you who did it.
　It was them.
　They're the ones.
　They're the ones who did it.
　They're the ones to be ashamed.
　And you're safe now. No one's going to harm you.
　No one's going to touch you.
　No one's going to hurt you now.
　Sssshhh. You're safe. You're safe.

RHODES. Brother. A successful day.

MUKHERJEE. No.

RHODES. On second thoughts . . . no. Not for you.
    Shame you couldn't keep your end up.
    But brother! Don't lose heart.
    There's always a second time.
    I'll sell you a hormone cream.
    The cure for all men's problems.
    Made by Playboy!
    Brother I despair of you.

THREE. And when Muntu returned

FOUR. Kali had gone.

    FOUR *becomes* MEENA.

MEENA. Where have you been?

MUNTU. Looking for you.

MEENA. I was here. Stupid. Put the water down.
    Now get out. This is no place for you.
    Sita. Let me wash you. Sita don't be ashamed.
    Sita I understand. Sita they did it to me.
    They took me to the city.
    They took me when I was just a little girl
    They locked me in this room
    It had a wooden floor and clean white walls
    Quite a pleasant room. It seemed so rich to me.
    A woman came. She had the hardest eyes.
    She looked me up and down. She said: "You'll do.
    Take off your clothes". And then she washed me.
    As if I was a kind of stone. And then she smiled.
    "New clothes", she said. "Pretty. Pretty clothes."
    They were all in white. I thought they were a present.
    And when the man came I still did not really understand. It all
    seemed like a dream.

    He pushed me on the bed. He tore off my pretty clothes. He
    lay on me.
    What are you doing? Why are you hurting me?
    He made me bleed. He made me bleed inside.

    The next one I did not obey.
    They had to tie me down.
    And then they took away my food.
    I had to do my quota or they took away my food.
    I had to do it willingly or else I'd starve.
    I had to smile.

And I had to eat. All of us must eat.
Their father always came. He was a regular.
Always on his trips to the city.
Mr Mukherjee. A most important man,
Very respectable.
Later I learnt that he'd arranged my sale.
With my father dead, my mother ill,
There'd been no one left to work the fields.
The rent had not been paid,
He was owed some money, and I cleared the debt.
But I lived, Sita. I lived. Life goes on.

ONE. Soon afterwards the brother left.

RHODES. There were tin openers going cheap. Electric tin
openers. From Detroit!

THREE. And life went on as before.

SITA. I woke each day with vomit in my mouth.

MUNTU. I beat the clothes.
I beat the clothes against the stones!

MUKHERJEE. But my clothes were never clean!

MEENA. All the fire went out of her.
She worked with downcast eyes.

MUNTU. Weeks passed. Weeks and weeks!

SITA. The garden turned to weeds.

FIVE. And then the brother returned.

RHODES. Brother you don't look cheerful.
What's so wrong?

MUKHERJEE. Life has not been good to me.

RHODES. But brother when I left everything was going so
well.

MUKHERJEE. Things were bad then. And now they're worse.

RHODES. But I gave you light!

MUKHERJEE. All the lights are broken. They were broken
months ago. The boys use them as target practice for their
stones.

RHODES. Is that all? Is that all that became of the light?

I give you the land and you let it go to waste.
I give you light and you do nothing with it.

MUKHERJEE. That is life.

RHODES. It's nothing to do with life!
What do you think life is?

MUKHERJEE. Life is an order that has been lost.

RHODES. Life is a market where you buy and sell.
And if you do nothing then you lose.
You lose everything.
Brother what an opportunity you have lost!

MUKHERJEE. Then why didn't you stay?

RHODES. I had other business.
You think a man like me can be confined to a village? I
travelled, brother. I did deals.
I lay with beautiful women. And I have come back laden with
good things.
Don't you want to see them?
Have you no curiosity?

MUKHERJEE. Brother I am ill! My stomach aches. Each night I
vomit blood.

RHODES. Call a doctor.

MUKHERJEE. There is no doctor!

RHODES. I'll sell you a pill.

MUKHERJEE. What's wrong with me cannot be cured with pills.
Pills don't wipe out crimes!

RHODES. You still feel guilt?

MUKHERJEE. Am I not right?

RHODES. Guilt is useless.

MUKHERJEE. Brother she is now with child!

RHODES. That's no concern of mine.

MUKHERJEE. Your child.

RHODES. How can it be mine?

MUKHERJEE. You raped her.

RHODES. I taught her a lesson. She probably enjoyed it.
And if I caused her pain,

I'm sure she'll have forgotten that.
Watch brother. I'll call her. And we'll see
Sita, Sita!

Enter SITA *with downcast eyes*.

RHODES. See brother I call and she comes
As she always did.
Now Sita. Smile. Smile Sita. Smile!
Don't be so selfish.
Smile at my brother. Cheer him up.
He's feeling sad.
There. See brother.
It was just a carnival excess
Forgiven and forgotten.
Does she work well?

MUKHERJEE. She is always sick!

RHODES. Don't be sick, Sita.
There's no need to be sick.
Life goes on. Just as before.
Perhaps more peacefully
For now you won't be troubled with any thoughts of gaining
land.
By unwise thoughts and crazy dreams
Or having futile talks with lawyers.

SITA. I saw the lawyer. That very day.
I walked all day by the edge of the road.
Huge lorries thundered past.
I had to stop and rest. I get so tired!
When I reached the office it was afternoon.
There was a crowd of people there.
He worked into the night.
I sat in a fetid room
And I listened to the children crying.
At last the room was empty and my turn came.

ONE *becomes the* LAWYER.

I am Sita, Muntu's wife.
We took your advice.
We dug the ground.
They raped me in the village square
And now I'm pregnant
This will be their child!

LAWYER. Sita I'm sorry. I am so very sorry.
I gave you bad advice. But I acted for the best.
There is nothing I can do.
Sita I have empty hands!
Have you seen the people waiting?
Have you seen the misery in that room?
There is a village, Sita,
Not so far from here.
A village so poor it has no name.
They are bringing their children
They are bringing them to the doctor
– who can do nothing! –
They are waiting at the clinic
And then they are waiting to see me.
There are children there with double thumbs
Children born that have no mouths or ears
Others have triple rows of teeth
Many vomit all the time
Most are tired and weak.
They have monstrous growths that eat away their skins.
Monstrous growths that never heal.
No one knows what causes this.
Some say it is the water.
Others say it is carried in the air.
Others blame the electricity.
They are ignorant people.

Go to the lawyer, they all say,
He will help you. He is the people's friend.
He will fight for you.
He will give you compensation.
But how can I compensate for poisoned lives?
And how can I fight?
I am just one man
In a dirty office with worm-eaten books.
My only weapon is the law. A broken sword!
The law is such a fragile thing
And it is broken. Broken beyond repair.
It has become just another tool the powerful use.
They use it as it pleases them.
And they will not stand for opposition.
They want to kill me. Even me!
Even a helpless person such as I!
No one will guard me. Everyone is too afraid.

You are in danger sitting here.
My only advice to you is leave.
I wanted to help, Sita.
I always wanted suffering to end.
But each day brings more people waiting.
More people standing at my door.
And I am helpless.
It is a tide, Sita, a rising tide of suffering
And in this tide of human misery
This rising tide
Yours is just a trivial case.
Forgive me but I cannot help.

SITA. Then I lost all hope
And so I stand and serve these men
And try to imagine that I'm somewhere else.

RHODES. Won't you talk, Sita?
Why have you gone so surly?
You're worse than my brother.
You need cheering too.
Come I'll show you something. Come.
You remember the trinkets that I used to bring?
The bracelets and the shiny scarves?
I gave you bracelets, Sita.
And a necklace once. Do you remember?
Things are better now. I've prospered.
Look. Fully portable, 14 inch screen,
NICAM stereo built-in volume control.
Fully automatic! My first television!
I told you I was doing well.

MUKHERJEE. Stolen fire.

RHODES. Brother?

MUKHERJEE. I tell you this is stolen fire.

RHODES. Don't be so foolish brother. I have a licence.

MUKHERJEE. Prometheus.

RHODES. Who's he?

MUKHERJEE. A giant.

RHODES. Is he jolly? Is he green?

MUKHERJEE. No.

RHODES. American?

MUKHERJEE. Greek.

RHODES. There's nothing he can say to us.
  Watch this, brother. This!
  This will be a wonder!

MUKHERJEE. He gave man the gift of fire.
  He stole it from the gods.
  Fire was a gift the gods had kept from men.
  And men lived in ignorance of it.
  They lived a peaceful life. They tended flocks.
  Sometimes when lightning struck a tree they'd take the burning
  branch and try to keep the fire alive.
  They worshipped it, but did not know the secret of its use.
  But he gave it them. He taught them the use of ovens, and the
  smelting of brass. He taught them to build villages and towns.
  He taught them the secrets of the foundry and the forge.
  And so they prospered. But it was stolen fire: and so they came
  to harm.
  They fought over the spoils.
  They burnt down their villages.
  They torched their crops.
  They melted down their ploughshares and they turned them
  into swords.
  They used the forge to sharpen instruments of war
  Instruments to maim and kill
  And what was given us for good was turned to harm.

RHODES. Oh brother. How moral. How very very moral.

MUKHERJEE. Prometheus was punished by the gods.
  He was nailed to a cliff with his face to the burning sun.
  Stakes were driven through his feet and hands.
  He suffered agonies of thirst.
  Each day an eagle came to tear out his guts
  And each night they grew whole again.
  So his agony was repeated over and over
  Over and over to the very end of time.

RHODES. You've got the wrong story brother. You're the one
  with the stomach ache.
  There, Sita, there!
  Now look! Pictures from America!

TWO. And Sita looked into the magic screen and saw

THREE. The real thing

ONE. Performance without compromise

FOUR. New Kids On The Block

ONE. News at Ten

FOUR. Madonna

THREE. Cola you can trust

FOUR. Only Smarties have the answer.

MUKHERJEE. There once were gods who walked the earth.
   There were spirits in the rivers and the trees.
   That's what I'll believe. Not this.
   This is the age of lies.
   We've lost our innocence.

RHODES. Brother there never was a golden age,
   There never was a time of peace and plenty,
   A time before the beginning of war.
   There's always been war. Wars and more wars.
   Brother, that's what we call history.
   It's not the history of people or of progress or of kings. It's the
history of war.
   Wars over territories. Wars over gold.
   Wars over ideas. Wars for peace, brother.
   Wars for the truth.
   But nobody gives a shit for peace. Or cares a toss for truth.
   What they want is Coca Cola.
   Peace and plenty. Supermarkets. Wimpy bars and instant whip.
   And they are right! Who'd want hunger?
   Who would want disease?
   Who wants a life of endless grinding labour?
   Who wants to walk ten miles for firewood if they can cook with
the flick of a switch?
   Who wants to grind the stubborn corn?
   Who wants to dig the stony ground?

   Brother you have never worked. Never used your hands.
   Never felt weary, never felt hungry.
   Never felt the grinding boredom of the physical task.
   No one wants that, brother. No one wants to suffer.
   We all want this.
   Peace and prosperity. Popcorn in a bag!
   Nothing can stop it, brother. It's irresistible. .

It bounces off satellites, it flows silently down wires.
You can't keep it out with fences, or shut it out with walls.
It spreads everywhere. There's no escaping it.
The new and golden age. The age of light.
The new world order. The end of history.
Brother!

MUKHERJEE. I won't hear you. I won't!

RHODES. Pity. But he wouldn't have understood.
You might. Irresistible conquest.
It's a conquest you'll appreciate. The end of history. Aren't you
impressed?

SITA. It's all a different world.

RHODES. No, Sita. It is all one world.
All of us share the same world.
The old boundaries just aren't there any more.
All the walls are broken.
Think of it Sita! Think of the possibilities!

SITA. We haven't any water.

RHODES. What?

SITA. We've no clean water.
There's no one to mend the pump!

RHODES. No. You haven't seen the possibilities.
You can't even begin! You can't even begin to imagine!
I can.
I could have you Sita.
I could have you again.
I could have you any time I want.
Any time I choose. Any time.
But I don't want Sita. And I don't choose.
You're disgusting.
You're all blown up like a balloon.
Your eyes used to shine like hidden fires.
Now they're dull and lifeless.
Dead and glassy like a doll.
A cheap doll. A broken doll.
Made in Taiwan. That no one will ever buy.
A doll that no one wants to look at any more.
Sita. You've let yourself go.
You should be ashamed.
If your husband had any spunk in him he'd let you go.

He'd throw you out, Sita. Get rid of you.
You're a disgrace.
You should look after yourself.
Take more care. Take care of yourself.
Be like me. I take care. I exercise.
Look. I use it every day.
A bullworker. Made in America.

Exit RHODES. SITA *is sick. She weeps.* MUNTU *approaches
timidly.*

MUNTU. Wife. My wife. My beautiful wife. You shrink from me.
Why do you think from me? I don't mean you harm. I want to
take away your pain. I want to wash away your tears.

SITA. There's nothing you can wash away!

MUNTU. It's over. Sita it's all over.

SITA *shakes her head and retreats into herself.*

MUNTU. Sita don't go away. Come back! Speak to me!

SITA. What could I say?

MUNTU. I don't know. I don't care. Anything.
Anything you like.

SITA. I lost my voice.
I lost it when he stuffed it full of dirt.

MUNTU. All the dirt's been washed away.

SITA. My mouth is choked with dirt!
My ears my eyes each part of me so I can't feel or touch or be
aware of anything but dirt!
This feeling that I'm dirt!

MUNTU. It isn't true.

SITA. You're always saying that!

MUNTU. Why won't you believe me?

SITA. Because I can't! I can't!

MUNTU. I should have died. I should have died before I let
them do it.

SITA. You've told me that before. It makes no difference. It's far
too late.

MUNTU. Sita we'll have a child. A child we dreamed of.
A child!

SITA. A child?
  Muntu I have this thing inside of me
  A monster, Muntu, a stranger in my body
  A thing.
  A living thing
  A thing that makes me sick and weak and tired
  A hostile alien thing
  That's taken over my own flesh
  And made it not my own.
  I'd kill it if I could
  But it won't die.
  It just won't die!

MUNTU. Our child!

SITA. Muntu it's not our child!

MUNTU. It's Mother Kali's.

SITA. What?

MUNTU. She came back. She gave me back my dream.

SITA. Muntu they're over. Dreams are over.

MUNTU. That's why it all went wrong. Because I forgot the
  dream. I forgot the dream that Mother Kali sent me. I was too
  afraid. But I won't be afraid. Or at least I'll try. I won't because
  I want the child. I don't care who the father is. I'll believe she's
  ours. Otherwise we've nothing. Sita I know we're weak. I know
  that we're alone. But she won't be like that. She won't be like
  us. She won't be small and powerless and alone. She won't be
  weak. She won't be weary and afraid.
  Oh Sita listen. Don't close yourself. Don't shut your mind. That
  man is evil but we're not all the same. If we close ourselves
  we're lost. Sita come. Take my hand. My hand, Sita, my hand!

KALI. I destroyed a city once
  Where they raped a woman that I loved
  She said:

TWO. I know what you intend. You're right.
  It's a crime against love
  A crime against the heart.
  And that's the greatest crime of all
  So burn the city if you like
  Burn all of it.
  But burn me in it. Please. I'm so very tired.

Breathing disgusts me
And my body seems a heavy useless thing.

KALI. We were silent for a while.
  I held her in my arms. I tried to comfort her.
  And then she said:

TWO. But Kali, what about the children?

KALI. They're all infected.
  Their fathers beat them and their mothers too
  Beat them in a casual careless way
  As if it didn't matter.
  They'll all grow up to be the same.

TWO. But what if there's a hundred people there
  A hundred good and loving people
  Would you kill them too?
  Kill the good along with the bad?

KALI. Do you think there's a hundred people here?
  A hundred good and loving people?
  A hundred who deserve to live?

TWO. What if there were only ninety-nine?
  Would you kill them all just for the sake of one?

KALI. I don't expect there's even ninety-nine.
  They look a dubious set of bastards there to me.

TWO. And she brought it down and down right down to five.

KALI. They'll all die anyway.
  They can't escape the things they've done.

  And so I burnt the city. I burnt it to ash.
  But I let her go.
  I said "Don't you look back
  Do whatever you want but don't look back
  And don't feel pity".
  She was high on the hill
  She was high on the very last hill
  Another moment and she would have left the plains for ever.

  She suddenly recalled a distant friend
  She turned
  She looked
  She saw
  And what she saw then turned her heart to stone.

Mukherjee.

MUKHERJEE. Who is it?

KALI. Mukherjee.

MUKHERJEE. Go away.

KALI. I've come for you.

MUKHERJEE. Leave me alone.
Can't you see I'm ill?
I want to sleep.

KALI. But Mukherjee. You are asleep.

MUKHERJEE. Then let me be.

KALI. But I have news for you.

MUKHERJEE. What news?

KALI. You'll never wake.

And now you know me.
And now you are afraid.

MUKHERJEE. What do you want?

KALI. You know what I want.

MUKHERJEE. I've done nothing!

KALI. But Mukherjee you have.
Everyone has. Everyone's done something.

MUKHERJEE. Nothing bad!

KALI. Makes no difference.

MUKHERJEE. I'm a man of culture.

KALI. How very sad.

MUKHERJEE. Yes it has been sad! Living here in this desert.
I've tried to have an intellectual life
But no one's interested. No one cares.
Hardly anyone can read! Life is empty!

KALI. You poor man. How very sad. You poor rich.
Pity the rich.
Pity those with an educated turn of mind.
Pity the feeling and the sensitive. Poor rich.
How many children died so you could enjoy your sense of
emptiness?

The luxury of the educated mind. How many?

MUKHERJEE. None. None! I killed no one!

KALI. The children lie in the gutters and stare
At the rich in their towers of sculptured glass
And the rich ignore them
Or feel self-righteous if they spare a tiny crust.
Prisoners in their towers of glass
Prisoners afraid to feel the rain
Forgetting it's the earth brings forth their food
Living life as if it were an endless credit card
Forgetting that in the end they pay for it.
For they must pay. Everyone has to pay.
Pity the rich Mukherjee. Pity the rich.
Watch them as they suffer stress
In pursuit of leather three piece suites
And designer labels on their leisure clothes.
They wade through blood and hunger and disease
And buy deodorants so they won't suffer from the smell.
Precious people Mukherjee. Refined people of sensitivity and
taste.
And don't tell me you're poor.
Don't tell me of the comforts that you lack.
I look at what you have and how you squandered it.

MUKHERJEE. I did my best.

KALI. Everyone does their best. It isn't good enough!

MUKHERJEE. What else can we do?

KALI. Have pity. Love.

MUKHERJEE. I loved my father.

KALI. It isn't enough.

MUKHERJEE. Can no one help me?

KALI. No one, Mukherjee. There is no help.
No help at all.

KALI *puts a bag over* MUKHERJEE's *head and strangles him. She removes the bag, arranges the body.* SITA *watches. Their eyes meet. A moment.* KALI *takes out a knife and approaches* SITA.

SITA. I am not afraid.

KALI. I haven't come for you.
I'm the woman in your husband's dream.

I gave him a child.
This is what I give to you.

She gives her the knife.

SITA. I don't want to kill.

KALI. But Sita there is no other way to live.
And death don't matter.
It's only life that counts.

Exit KALI. SITA *is left with the knife.*

SITA. Sita is lost in the forest, so the story goes,
Or Sita is imprisoned in her island jail.
Demons surround her. She is all alone.
She waits and she waits for her hero to come
For her Prince to come and take her from the tower.
She waits and she waits and she waits and waits.
And no one comes.
And I want to weep. But there is no use in that.
There are no heroes any more.
There's just ourselves.

Enter RHODES.

RHODES. Sita my brother's died! How selfish of him. He could
have waited till I'd gone. Inconsiderate!
Now I'll have to bury him. I'll have to find a priest! Are there
any? Are there any priests?
Sita I was watching a precision bombing raid. Surgical strike!
Laser guided targets!
And learning about an electric hand grenade!
No more old-fashioned clinks and bumps.
No more antique percussion pins.
This is ignited by electric charge.
Completely silent! With a reliability of 98.7 percent! And it
scatters bomblets all around! Plastic fragments invisible to
X-rays. Three thousand fragments! And it only weighs two
pounds!
And if you've got the money you can order it!
Hallett and Waly Didcott, Derbyshire!
They accept all major credit cards!
And we cannot afford them. It isn't fair!
All this is theirs while we stagnate in poverty!
What's to be done, Sita, what's to be done to change this? It's
an injustice.
Something must be done! What can we do?

He has got very close to her.

SITA. We just make do with knives.

She castrates him.

KALI. It was just a little cut
   Through two tiny knobs of flesh
   Two wrinkled bags.

SITA. At first he couldn't believe it.
   He couldn't believe what I had done to him
   And then he understood. He made this noise.
   I put a stop to it.
   It was distracting me.

She stabs him again and he dies. She looks at him a while.

SITA. It was such a little knife.
   I never knew that they could be so small.

FOUR. And she put down the knife

ONE. And she closed his eyes

FOUR. And left the house behind.

ONE. She walked out to the field

THREE. Where her husband was staring at the wasted land.

FOUR. The tiny barren patch of ground.

ONE. The dew was wet in the grass.

FOUR. Mist was rising from the river.

ONE. It was the hour of dawn.

SITA. Muntu.
   Don't tell me what I should have done.
   Don't tell me that I should forgive.
   Look at the earth Muntu. The wasted earth.
   The garden that we dreamed of
   Has turned into a barren patch of weeds.
   Muntu we'll dig the ground.
   We'll clear it and we'll plant our seeds.
   They'll tell us it's a waste of time.
   That others will come to take away our land.
   Or else they'll come to imprison me.
   Some seeds will fall on stony ground.
   Others will be eaten by the birds.

And some will be choked and smothered by the weeds
But I won't believe they'll all be lost
Or that our labour will be wasted.
This moment is the only thing we've got.
There's nothing else. We'll dig. We'll dig!